# MARRIAGE'S LITTLE
## ADVICE BOOK

Also by Bill and Gloria Adler

*The Joys of Having a Child*

# MARRIAGE'S LITTLE ADVICE BOOK

## ADVICE BOOK

❧

*Bill and Gloria Adler*

William Morrow and Company, Inc.
New York

Library of Congress Cataloging-in-Publication Data

Adler, Bill.
    Marriage's little advice book / Bill Adler, Gloria Adler.
        p.    cm.
    ISBN 0-688-12396-1
    1. Marriage—Miscellanea.    I. Adler, Gloria    II. Title.
    HQ734.A245    1994
    646.7′8—dc20                                                    93-38290
                                                                          CIP

Printed in the United States of America

First Edition

1 2 3 4 5 6 7 8 9 1

BOOK DESIGN BY LISA STOKES

To both newlyweds and old hands at marriage. . .

and to Peggy and Bill junior for Karen and Claire and to Diane and Shawn for Madeleine

# $\mathcal{P}$reface

We were married on February 26, 1956. That was thirty-seven years ago and still counting.

This book is the result of thirty-seven years of a marriage that has worked and of two people who are more in love than they were when they took their marriage vows.

It is our hope that some of the thoughts and words in this book will help and inspire newlyweds—those about to be married— and those who have been married for a longer period of time.

Bill and Gloria Adler

Never go to bed mad.

Never wake up mad.

Compromise!

Don't believe everything you see and
hear on *Donahue*.

Be a good listener.

Share the kitchen chores.

Be careful of bad breath.

Say "I love you" at least three times a day and more on the weekend.

Remember, there never was and there never will be such a thing as a "perfect marriage."

Accept your mate for what they are—
not what you would like them to be.

Have separate checking accounts.

Run, walk, swim, jog, exercise together.

Love your spouse's parents as if they
were your own.

Talk with each other instead of turning on TV.

Have spontaneous sex.

Remember your mate's birthday and never forget your anniversary.

Be a sympathetic listener.

Hug! Hug! Hug!

Don't be jealous of your mate's past flings.

Remember, the first twenty-five years of marriage are only practice. The next twenty-five are the real fun.

Keep your mate healthy.

If you were a slob when you were a kid
and your mother used to pick up after
you, don't expect your mate to do the
same thing.

Try not to snore.

Have a candlelight dinner once a
month for just the two of you.

Sneak away to a motel for a weekend.

Talk things out.

Don't be the one who doesn't replace the toilet paper when it runs out.

Cook a surprise dinner for your mate—even if you've never cooked before.

Compliment your mate at least twice a day.

Say "thank you" even if you are married—and "please."

Invite your mate's parents over for dinner.

Don't try to be romantic before you
brush your teeth.

Never tell your mate everything!

Start a hobby you can share together.

Get the video and watch *Casablanca*
together.

Never lie.

Be your mate's best friend.

Always be there when your mate
needs you.

Wash your mate's back once a week.

Go to your mate's class reunion but don't make any sarcastic remarks.

Hug your mate when they least expect it.

Don't have just his or her friends— have friends you share.

SEND BIRTHDAY FLOWERS
TO YOUR MOTHER·IN·LAW.

Don't keep your mate on a tight leash.

Share a song that is your song.

Watch your table manners even if you
and your mate are eating alone.

Don't be ashamed to cry in front of
your mate.

Knock before you enter the bathroom
if the door is closed.

Buy a surprise gift for your mate even
if it costs less than five dollars. It really
is the thought that counts.

Give your mate space.

Never be jealous of somebody else's marriage.

Rich people don't have happier marriages.

Once a year repeat your marriage vows.

If your mate isn't in the mood, don't press.

Never fight over which TV program to watch. Read a book instead.

Call your mate's mother on the spur of the moment just to say "hello."

Never open your mate's mail. Respect their privacy.

Don't be shy about telling your mate if there is a problem when you are making love.

Respect your mate's desire for peace and quiet.

Do something special for your mate
even if it is something silly.

Kiss and make up even if you haven't
had a fight.

Visit the spot where you first met.

Hold hands even if you are alone in
your home.

Discuss your financial problems *before*
they become a crisis.

Laugh a lot together.

Remember, marriages that last are
based on love, trust, and a lot of luck.

Pray together.

Visit the old neighborhood where your mate grew up.

Every day remember  why you married your mate.

Help your mate keep their cholesterol down.

Write a love letter to your mate each
year on your anniversary.

Leave a love note under your mate's
pillow.

Be punctual. Don't keep your mate
waiting.

Share a great book you are reading.

Read aloud to each other.

Take a vacation where your mate
wants to go every other year.

Keep a picture of your mate in your
wallet or purse, or on your desk at the
office.

Don't be a bigger spender than your mate.

Make a list of all the things you love about your mate and look at it every now and then.

Be the first to say "I'm sorry."

Have a celebration even if there is no reason for one.

Keep boredom out of your marriage. Do the unexpected.

Make new friends who you can enjoy together.

Take lots of pictures of your trips, your parties, your family, your friends. Good memories are important.

Talk out your problems—even if it takes all week.

Control your temper.

Don't leave the garbage for your mate
to take out.

Don't be afraid to say "I was wrong."

If your mate is driving the car, don't be
a backseat driver.

Share a joke.

Dim the lights, put on some music, and dance.

Don't criticize your mate in front of family or friends.

Keep your bad habits to yourself. Don't pass them on to your mate.

SPLURGE! HAVE A FINE ARTIST
DO A PAINTING OF YOUR MATE.

Snack on popcorn together. There are practically no calories.

Talk sofly to each other instead of shouting.

If you are out of town, call your mate before you go to sleep.

Don't walk around the house nude unless you really look good in the nude. (Most people don't.)

Don't wear makeup all the time, especially around the house. Look natural.

If your mate doesn't like your perfume, change it. (Ask him.)

Don't interrupt your mate when they are talking.

Try to be more romantic now than you were on your honeymoon.

Leave funny, romantic, silly, loving messages on your mate's answering machine.

If you are really mad, take a long walk around the block before you say anything.

If you are married to a person who is a great carpenter, electrician, and plumber, thank your lucky stars!

Don't try to always get your own way.

Watch what you eat—and watch what
your mate eats.

Take care of something together—a
child, a pet, or even a plant.

Before you have a fight, remember
how silly the last fight was.

Compliment your mate even if it is about something minor.

Don't be too stubborn to say "It was my fault."

Don't be the one to leave the dirty dishes in the sink so they are there the next morning when you and your mate get up.

Make friends with other couples who have good marriages.

Don't be too stubborn to lose an argument.

Don't be too stubborn to change.

Save the last chocolate in the box for the one you love.

Try to make your marriage a little
better each and every day.

Help your mate succeed in business.

Find a couple who have been happily
married for fifty years and ask them
their secret.

Find at least a day and a night each week when you and your mate can be alone together.

Send funky greeting cards to your mate even if there is no special occasion.

Start each day with thanks for your mate.

If it was your fault, ask to be forgiven.
If it was your mate's fault, forget it.

Be faithful.

Don't spend so much time at the office
that you hardly see or talk to your
mate.

Always leave time for making love.

Nobody's perfect. Not your mate. Not even you.

Treat every moment of your marriage as if it were priceless.

Go for an impulsive walk in the rain together.

Share the pleasures of nature—a nice stroll in the park or a hike up a mountain.

Don't try to run your mate's life.

Know your mate's medical history in case of an emergency.

Know your mate's size so when you
buy something, it will fit.

Expect a lot but be ready to gladly and
happily accept less.

Give more to your marriage than you
receive.

Don't argue in front of strangers.

SNEAK A PEEK AT YOUR MATE
WHEN THEY ARE FAST ASLEEP.
IT'S A WONDERFUL SIGHT.

Make yours a Tiffany marriage even if you are on a Kmart budget.

Always compromise.

Share a fine bottle of wine for no special reason.

Three little words—"I love you"—are magical.

Don't surprise your mate by inviting unexpected guests.

Don't compare your marriage to your parents' marriage.

The silent types usually wind up living alone.

Remember your marriage vows as if they were the Ten Commandments.

Be generous with love and frugal with money.

Sneak a peek at your mate when they are fast asleep. It's a wonderful sight.

Share your joys.

Share your sorrows (that is, after all, what a mate is for).

Don't fall asleep while your mate is talking to you.

Don't bother to read all the magazine articles on how to make your marriage work. Better to use your common sense.

Kiss your mate when they least
expect it.

Celebrate every anniversary as if it
were your first!

Don't tell jokes at the expense of your
mate.

You be the one to get the mouse in the cellar.

If your mate puts a dent in the car, act as if it isn't there.

Don't let your marriage get boring.

Trust keeps a marriage together.

Don't embarrass your mate by getting drunk in public.

Share your favorite ice cream.

If you have made out a will, don't keep it a secret.

Never lend money to your mate's relatives.

Read to each other from your favorite book.

Every now and then, wear sexy underwear.

First become best friends—then become lovers.

Do something impulsively romantic at least once a month.

Never compare your mate to your mother or your father.

A good mattress is an important contribution to a good marriage.

Don't try to dominate your mate.

In a marriage, there is no substitute for mutual respect.

Don't bring the job into the bedroom.

Share the telephone equally.

Tell your mate when the lovemaking was great.

Don't hog all the closet space.

Never let marriage problems fester. Solve them as quickly as you can.

Leave the bathroom neat and clean for your mate.

Be there when your mate needs you.

Don't be stingy with compliments.

Show your affection. Don't hide it.

Hold hands in public places—
especially in public places.

Never stop wooing your mate.

Don't ask your mate to give up their friends.

Take out your wedding album and relive your wedding.

Watch your wedding video.

Talk about your future together.

Don't always have dinner in a restaurant with other people. Dine out alone, just you two.

Celebrate your first thousand hours of marriage with a bottle of champagne.

Freeze what is left of your wedding cake to finish on your one-month anniversary.

Treat your mate to breakfast in bed.

Brag about your mate.

Take a moonlight swim once a year.

Shower together every now and then.

Keep a diary of the wonderful
moments you never want to forget.

REMEMBER YOUR WEDDING
VOWS AS IF THEY WERE
THE TEN COMMANDMENTS.

Share a favorite flower.

Don't be the one who uses up the
toothpaste and doesn't replace it.

Fight fair.

Have your own little secret that only
the two of you know.

Don't pay the bills just before you are going to make love.

Send your father-in-law a birthday card.

If you are a better cardplayer than your mate, lose on purpose every now and then.

Money ruins more relationships than
infidelity.

Never try to make love after you have
had too much to drink.

Remember it takes two to fight but
only one to make up.

Take an adult-education class together.

Plant a tree and watch it grow year by year together.

Adopt a pet from the ASPCA.

Keep your temper to yourself.

Don't fight over politics.

Always look for the silver lining.

Keep a photographic record of your marriage's happiest moments.

Don't invest your mate's money in the stock market.

Learn CPR in case your mate is in trouble.

Try listening.

Don't be a complainer.

Count your blessings—instead of counting money.

Pay your bills the same time as your mate does.

Turn off the TV when you are having dinner at home so you can talk.

Make sure your mate uses the seat belt.

Remind your mate to visit the dentist.

Always let your mate know they are
appreciated.

Ask your mate not to exceed the speed
limit.

Try not to take phone calls when you
are having dinner together.

Don't ask your friends for advice
about your marriage—they are having
their own problems.

Nobody wants to be married to a nag.

If you have to stay late at the office, try to warn your mate beforehand.

Share the Sunday papers.

Don't ask too many questions.

Don't begin an argument with the words "My parents would never . . ."

Don't plan your marriage around your horoscope.

Don't let a day go by without working on improving your relationship.

Don't spy.

Too many possessions in a marriage can possess the marriage.

Be as well informed as your mate.

Don't keep secrets.

Don't make your mate have to be the one to change all the clocks when it becomes daylight saving time.

Visit the zoo together.

Your mate should be your hero.

Instead of thinking that 50 percent of marriages end in divorce, think that 50 percent of marriages live happily ever after.

Don't tell your best friend anything you wouldn't tell your mate.

Don't spend time talking on the phone
with your parents—when you should
be talking to your mate.

Ride on a bicycle built for two.

Always check the joint tax return
before you sign it.

DON'T USE YOUR MATE'S
RAZOR.

Share the good times but be willing to
share the bad times too.

Let your mate sleep late on Sunday
while you make breakfast.

Show you care.

Compromise 365 days a year.

When talking to your mate on the telephone, never put them on hold.

Don't get drunk at your mate's
Christmas party.

Think of your mate before you think
of yourself.

Every now and then read an erotic book out loud to each other.

Never miss the chance to tell your mate you love them.

Don't try to make your mate your servant or maid.

Negotiate your differences.

Romance your mate all over again.

There is no such thing as a perfect marriage, but if you work at it, you can come close.

Let your mate know you care by deeds—not just words.

Never make a promise you don't
intend to keep.

Never lie to your mate. Never!

Share your baby pictures with
your mate.

Be romantic when your mate doesn't
expect it.

Communicate your feelings.

Don't go to bed with cold feet.

Pay your bills on time.

Never discuss bad news first thing in
the morning or last thing at night.

In a happy marriage, neither partner is superior.

Fax your mate a love poem.

Be sensitive with your mate.

Flirt with each other.

Share a bag of Hershey's Kisses.

Snuggle.

Never be so stubborn that you are not willing to compromise.

Visit Disney World together.

Fall head over heels in love every single day.

Wash your car together.

Encourage your mate to have a night
out with friends without you.

Be lovable.

Share the same New Year's resolution.

Share a hot tub.

Kiss and make up.

Don't be moody.

Share an evening with the friends who got you together.

Buy your mate a gift you really can't afford (at least once).

Read Shakespeare's *Romeo and Juliet*
out loud.

Count your blessings.

Talk about your previous relationships.

Take the phone off the hook so you can
really be alone.

❧

Have faith in your mate.

Be devoted.

Do a really tough crossword puzzle
together.

Spend some time away from each
other.

Celebrate the anniversary of the first day you met.

Listen to the advice of people who have stayed happily married— not those who have split.

Never forget why you married in the first place.

It's the small things in marriage that count—like emptying the dishwasher.

Don't crowd your mate.

Furniture doesn't make a home—love does.

Do unto your mate as you would want your mate to do unto you.

Fill your marriage with lots of laughter.

Try a warm embrace.

There is no such thing as too much love.

Always be there when they need you.

EVERY NOW AND THEN WEAR
SEXY UNDERWEAR.

A word spoken in anger would be
better off not said.

Kind words are worth more than
jewels.

Don't eavesdrop when your mate is on
the phone.

The best things in marriage are free—
like hugs, kisses, and love.

Massage your mate's feet.

Don't ever put down your mate.

Share your innermost thoughts.

If your mate hurts, share the pain.

Be willing to compromise—seven days a week, fifty-two weeks a year, twenty-four hours a day.

Ask your mate to marry you all over again.

Have a romantic nickname for your mate.

Don't use your mate's razor.

If your mate doesn't want to talk about it—don't press.

Have a midnight champagne supper.

Forgive your mate as you would want to be forgiven.

Share a beautiful sunrise—no matter how early in the morning.

Learn the Heimlich maneuver. You never know.

Study a foreign language together.

Revisit the place where you spent your wedding night.

Always give your mate the benefit of the doubt.

Be your mate's confidant.

Be your mate's shrink.

Make your mate feel wanted.

Don't pout.

Don't hold a grudge.

Don't make a major problem out of a minor problem.

Never go back on your word.

Enjoy the simple pleasures together— the trees, the grass, the flowers, the sun, and the stars.

Never miss the chance to tell your
mate you love them.

Each and every day find a way to make
your marriage just a little better.

Don't be embarrassed to tell your mate
what turns you on.

Save an hour a day just for talking.

Don't leave the water running for the
next person to turn off.

Revisit the church or temple where
you were married and say hello to the
minister or rabbi who married you.

Comfort your mate when they hurt.

Don't be lazy about your chores
around the house.

You should both know how to use the
vacuum cleaner.

Learn to like *Monday Night Football*
for your mate's sake.

Don't cut things out of the newspaper before your mate has had a chance to read it.

Don't use all the hot water for your shower. Save some for your mate.

Never tell your mate you can't go out because you have nothing to wear.

Don't drink the last cold beer or eat the
last kiwi.

Don't hog the blankets.

Don't encourage the cat to sleep with
the two of you.

Buy a lottery ticket together.

Don't count on your mate to always
balance the checkbook.

Don't argue over who gets the crossword puzzle first.

Don't rearrange the furniture without
discussing it first.

DON'T INVITE THE CAT OR DOG
INTO BED UNLESS YOUR
MATE AGREES.

Invite your mother-in-law for the weekend.

Don't hog the remote control.

Don't be embarrassed to cry at the movies.

Make sure your mate eats enough fruits and vegetables.

Don't let your mate drive the car after drinking.

Give your mate a surprise fortieth birthday party.

Show affection.

Compromise even if you have already compromised that day.

Let your mate know how smart you think they are.

Trust each other.

Keep the promises you made to each other *before* you got married.

Don't be jealous.

It's better to get mad and get it over with than to get mad and keep it bottled up.

Make sure your mate eats broccoli.

Have faith in God—and each other.

Be in the same shape on your twenty-fifth anniversary as you were on your wedding day.

Look for the silver lining.

Never keep your mate waiting longer than eight minutes.

Sing a duet together in the shower.

Hug after breakfast.

Keep a *marriage* photo album.

Don't con your mate.

Ride the roller coaster together.

If your mate doesn't want to tell you, don't ask them again who they voted for.

Don't leave a half-empty beer bottle in the refrigerator.

Don't give your mate any stock tips.

Cherish the simple pleasures together.

Never make a decision when you are mad.

Feed your mate oat bran.

Always make your mate feel appreciated.

Share the chore of finding a parking spot.

Don't set your mate's best friend up
with a blind date.

Tell your mate you love their new hair-
style—even if you don't.

Take good care of the one you love.

Don't gamble with your mate's money.

Don't build your marriage on sex alone.

Bite your tongue before you are tempted to say something nasty.

Find time to listen.

Never use your mate's credit card without checking first.

Never storm out of the house when you are having an argument with your mate.

Splurge. Surprise your mate with caviar.

Don't be ashamed to say "It was my fault."

Praise your mate. Don't criticize.

Don't holler so the neighbors can hear.

Try tenderness.

Be enthusiastic about your mate's success.

Teach your mate how to ride a bike if they don't know already—so you can bike together.

Caring is part of loving.

True love is a gift very few people receive.

Take dancing lessons together. Learn the mambo.

Never kiss after eating garlic.

Read Dr. Seuss out loud together.

Never expect more from your mate than you are willing to give.

Be passionate.

Negotiate your differences.

Sin together!

Don't wear a real skimpy bathing suit
unless you check first with your mate.

YOU ARE NEVER TOO SOPHISTICATED
TO PLAY "SPIN THE BOTTLE"
(JUST THE TWO OF YOU, OF COURSE).

If you make more money than your mate, don't flaunt it.

Splurge.

Split a Sara Lee cake and don't worry about the calories.

Don't be the one to use the last clean towel.

Don't take too long in the bathroom in the morning if your mate is waiting.

Don't flirt when you go to cocktail parties.

Don't clean the house in the middle of the night.

Listen to your heart.

Never let your mate down.

Make a lifetime commitment.

Keep your word—always.

Fidelity.

Finish a crossword puzzle together.

Share the shopping at the supermarket.

Refill the ice cube tray so your mate
doesn't always have to do it.

Give up smoking for your mate.

Don't be a complainer.

Don't travel with more luggage than
your mate.

Don't try to dominate your mate.

Nobody wants to be with a
hypochondriac.

Kiss and make up.

Feed your mate well.

Don't compare your mate to Sean
Connery or Madonna.

Don't wear makeup to bed.

Keep your mate slim and trim.

If you are not prepared to compromise,
you probably should not be married.

Don't tell your mate what to wear.

Never betray your mate.

When you are both out of sorts, read
*Winnie-the-Pooh* together. It will make
you feel better.

Don't suggest kinky sex unless your mate really wants to.

Enjoy your differences and learn from them.

The real secret to a happy marriage is not finding the right mate but being the right mate.

Learn to accept each other's shortcomings.

Keep a positive attitude toward each other.

Respect and understand your mate's mood swings.

Don't be self-centered.

Never underestimate the healing power
of love.

Have an affair with your mate.

Celebrate your love for each other.

Every day of your marriage your
kisses should get longer and longer
and longer.

If you don't work at your marriage,
you may soon be out of work as far as
your marriage is concerned.

You and your mate should live on
love—not on credit.

Marriage is an equal partnership.
There is no chairman of the board.

Don't compare your marriage to any-
one else's. You never know what goes
on behind closed doors.

To get more out of marriage, give
more of yourself.

Laugh together. Cry together.

Don't build your marriage on material
things. Build your marriage on
spiritual things.

Before you blame your mate, think
first if you should blame yourself.

A good marriage is like a lovely plant.
It requires continual care and affection.

TRY NUDE DANCING.

Don't brag about the affairs you had before you were married.

A kiss "good morning" and a kiss "good night" is the perfect beginning and the perfect end to a married day.

If you're having trouble sleeping, don't wake your mate to tell them.

One rose given with love says more than words.

Take up a sport you can learn and play together.

Try slow dancing. Just the two of you at home.

Find little things to celebrate—like when you or your mate lose a pound.

The Duke of Windsor gave up a kingdom for the one he loved. What sacrifices have you made?

Set aside a specific time to discuss money so you are not talking about it all the time.

Never argue when you are eating dinner.

Have a snowball fight.

Write down the ten things you like best about your marriage—and read the list to your mate.

Send a note of thanks to your mate's parents for having your mate.

Write a love poem even if it doesn't rhyme.

Sometimes body language can say more than a thousand words.

One of the best things about marriage is never having to eat alone.

Saying "Forgive me" is as important as saying "I love you."

End every fight in less than twenty-four hours.

Do something wild and impulsive—
just the two of you.

Money can't buy happiness in marriage—but commitment can.

Treat every day of your marriage as if
it were your very first day.

The honeymoon should never end.

A premarital agreement is a sure sign that your marriage is starting with a lack of trust.

Physical attraction is what gets you together. Mutual respect is what keeps you together.

It really is the little things in marriage that count most.

Remember most crises are not as bad
as they first seem and they *will* pass.

Good manners are important for a
good marriage.

Live your marriage like you would
want your kids to live their marriage.

Survival in marriage is easy if you start with mutual respect, honesty, trust, and lots of love.

You can never love too much.

Enjoy your marriage as if it were the only marriage you will ever have.

Tell your parents your marriage is great.

Plan for the future.

Listen to your grandparents. They know more about how to make a marriage work than any marriage counselor.

Become addicted to each other.

If your mate smokes, help them kick the habit.

Ask your mate, "Is there anything I can do to make you happier?"

Nobody is happy married to a slob.

Don't marry if you are looking for a father or a mother.

There is no substitute for trust.

Listen. Don't tune out your mate.

Listen as much as you talk.

Share everything.

Don't ever be afraid to tell your mate your innermost thoughts.

Never try to convince your mate of anything before they have had breakfast.

Encourage your mate to pursue their dream.

Do volunteer work together.

Tell your mate you care.

Listen to your mate.

Every now and then ask your mate,
"Anything you want to tell me?"

Never ask your mate to do anything
you wouldn't do yourself.

Take long walks.

Don't argue about relatives.

Once a month dress up for dinner even
if just the two of you are dining alone
at home.

Make sure your mate gets a physical checkup once a year.

Bring out the devil in your mate.

Don't leave your dirty socks under the bed.

Make the honeymoon last forever and a day.

Compromise because it is the smart thing to do.

Wear your wedding rings so everybody will know you are in love.

Sometimes it is more romantic to sleep in the nude.

A good marriage never gets boring. A great marriage is always exciting.

Share your favorite pizza with all the trimmings.

Be an optimist about your marriage.

Take long walks together while the city sleeps.

Live your marriage as if Hollywood were going to make a movie about it.

Have a fine artist do a painting of your mate.

Learn to say "I love you" in three foreign languages—try French, Spanish, and Japanese.

Be cheerful at breakfast.

Take long walks together on Sunday,
when you are more relaxed, to talk
over your problems.

Have a picnic lunch on a beautiful
spring day.

Butter your mate's toast at breakfast.

Rent the video of *Love Story* and cry together as you watch.

Keep a diary of all the great things that have happened in your marriage.

Don't try to be romantic if you haven't shaved for two days.

Freshen your breath with a mouthwash
when you awaken.

Cherish the imperfections of your
relationship.

Read aloud the love letters you wrote
to each other.

Hang mistletoe—not just at Christmas.

Trust your mate with your life.

Say "yes" instead of "no."

Take a hayride.

Plan a small dinner party with people
who are as happily married as you are.

You are never too sophisticated to play "Spin the Bottle" (just the two of you, of course).

Cuddle! Smooch!

Discover something new about your mate every day.

Say "I love you" with your eyes.

SNACK ON POPCORN TOGETHER.
THERE ARE PRACTICALLY NO
CALORIES.

Never let your mate cry themselves to sleep.

Show your mate how to change a flat tire—just in case you're not available.

Act as if you were the only two people in love in the world.

Sometimes just act goofy together.

Make believe you are sweet sixteen
and this is your very first romance.

Share a fortune cookie.

Read the passages from your favorite
book to each other.

Don't be too serious.

Get up early and surprise your mate
with their favorite breakfast.

Don't argue over which movie to see—
go see both of them.

Tell your mate you appreciate them.

Work at making your marriage work.

Believe in your mate.

Try nude dancing.

Make your mate's happiness your
top priority.

Share little secrets.

Share funny stories.

Don't disappoint your mate.

Make every day count.

Share an electric blanket.

Don't argue on an empty stomach.

If your mate asks for an extra piece of cake, refuse.

Make your mate laugh every chance you get.

Don't try to make your mate perfect.

Plan a reunion for all the friends and relatives who were at your wedding.

Design your home for comfort—not for show.

Pamper your mate.

Reveal your deepest thoughts.

Help your mate make their dreams come true.

Keep a budget together.

A happy marriage will keep you young forever.

Start each day with a smile for your mate. End each day with a smile for your mate.

Display your wedding pictures in your home.

Keep your mate healthy.

Try to remember the very first time you kissed your mate.

Take a ferry ride to nowhere.

Watch the old Fred Astaire movies to
recapture your parents' childhood.

Admit your mate was right when your
mate was right.

Play some records from the sixties and
dance.

Sit on your mate's lap unexpectedly.

Make a valentine card instead of buying one.

Love your mate even when they are at their worst.

Lose five pounds for the one you love.

Kiss and make up *before* you fight.

Be intimate.

Anger destroys more marriages than infidelity.

Make a list of all the things you love about your mate and post it on the refrigerator.

Remember a good mate is hard to find.
A great one is a jewel.

Happily married people live longer.

Escape the city to a national park.

Kiss your mother-in-law as if you
mean it.

Don't reveal intimate details of your marriage, even to your best friend.

Make decisions in your marriage together.

It takes two people to make a marriage work.

Squeeze fresh orange juice for
your mate.

If your mate has a fear of the dentist,
go with them.

Make sure your mate practices sound
nutrition.

Keep your mate from drinking too
much.

Always be willing to try to understand
your mate's point of view.

Protect your mate.

Win your mate's heart each and every
day.

ᗗᘏᕱᗷ

Seduce your mate.

In a good marriage both partners are
equally strong.

Give your mate the best years of
your life.

Act out your fantasies with your mate.

Have fun gossiping about the neighbors.

Put a four-leaf clover next to your mate's night table.

Marriage means wanting to grow old together.

Vote for your mate for president.

Celebrate your mate's birthday with candles and champagne.

Hold hands for no reason at all.

Have your annual physical checkups together. That way you will be sure that your mate goes.

Soul kiss.

Go to sleep dreaming about your mate.
Wake up thinking about your mate.

Always have time for your mate.

Don't disappoint your mate.

Don't needle your mate about
their mistakes.

Don't look for perfection in your mate.

Spend quiet moments together.

Give more of yourself than you expect
to receive.

Save memorabilia from moments in
your marriage—like the napkin from
the first restaurant you went
to together.

Make friends with your mate's friends.

Don't spend your marriage as a couch
potato.

Start out each day of your married life
with a smile.

Run away together.

Believe in each other.

Make love on a secluded beach.

Take a cooking class together.

Have a dinner party for your mate's family.

Don't be a screamer.

Don't invite overnight houseguests without your mate's enthusiastic agreement.

Be romantic even without sex.

Leave a love note where your mate
would least expect to find it.

Share a barefoot walk along a
sandy beach.

Don't expect to live the way you did
when you lived alone.

On a bitterly cold day, put the heater
on in the car before your mate gets in.

Find the most difficult jigsaw puzzle
and finish it together.

Share the excitement of betting on a
horse in the Kentucky Derby.

Think about how wonderful it is to be
devoted to someone besides yourself.

Encourage your mate to do their
own thing.

Play hooky together.

Be enthusiastic about life—and
your marriage.

Be glad you have each other.

Do something nice for your mate without telling your mate you did it.

Laugh out loud a lot.

Find an old barn to make love in.

Life begins after you say "I do."

The most critical time in your marriage is breakfast time.

Remember the way your mate looked at you when you first met.

Close the closet doors.

A sense of humor in bed helps.

Don't always make love at the same time of day.

Rejoice in each other.

Go for a midnight bike ride together.

Share a box of Oreo cookies—and then go on a diet together.

Share intellectual pursuits.

Be a good listener.

Plan your future together—one day at a time.

Frame your wedding invitation and put it on your night table in the bedroom.

Be willing to let your mate have the last word.

Become each other's helpmate.

Research shows that you will live longer from a happy marriage than from eating fish.

Discover a small, intimate, inexpensive restaurant that can become "your place."

Don't hog the phone.

Revisit the spot where you first met.

Share the TV remote control.

Don't be embarrassed to be
sentimental.

Build your trust in each other one day
at a time.

There can never be too much love.

Try compromise before you try a marriage counselor.

All the marriage counselors in the world can't do as much good as three little words—"I love you."

Be willing to compromise seven days a week.

Send birthday flowers to your mother-in-law.

Invite your father-in-law to go fishing.

Don't have a baby to try to save your marriage.

Ask your mate out for a date like you used to do when you were courting.

Put imagination into your romantic moments.

Throw a surprise party for your mate
on your anniversary.

In marriage it's the little things that
you do for each other that mean a lot.

The very best mate is the one you are
married to.

Have a good cry together.

Have a good laugh together—often!

Pass this book on to a newlywed couple.